IPHIGENIA

BY P. SETH BAUER

DRAMATISTS
PLAY SERVICE
INC.

IPHIGENIA
Copyright © 2006, P. Seth Bauer

All Rights Reserved

CAUTION: Professionals and amateurs are hereby warned that performance of IPHIGENIA is subject to payment of a royalty. It is fully protected under the copyright laws of the United States of America, and of all countries covered by the International Copyright Union (including the Dominion of Canada and the rest of the British Commonwealth), and of all countries covered by the Pan-American Copyright Convention, the Universal Copyright Convention, the Berne Convention, and of all countries with which the United States has reciprocal copyright relations. All rights, including professional/amateur stage rights, motion picture, recitation, lecturing, public reading, radio broadcasting, television, video or sound recording, all other forms of mechanical or electronic reproduction, such as CD-ROM, CD-I, DVD, information storage and retrieval systems and photocopying, and the rights of translation into foreign languages, are strictly reserved. Particular emphasis is placed upon the matter of readings, permission for which must be secured from the Author's agent in writing.

The English language stock and amateur stage performance rights in the United States, its territories, possessions and Canada for IPHIGENIA are controlled exclusively by DRAMATISTS PLAY SERVICE, INC., 440 Park Avenue South, New York, NY 10016. No professional or nonprofessional performance of the Play may be given without obtaining in advance the written permission of DRAMATISTS PLAY SERVICE, INC., and paying the requisite fee.

Inquiries concerning all other rights should be addressed to Robert A. Freedman Dramatic Agency, Inc., 1501 Broadway, Suite 2310, New York, NY 10036. Attn: Marta Praeger.

SPECIAL NOTE

Anyone receiving permission to produce IPHIGENIA is required to give credit to the Author as sole and exclusive Author of the Play on the title page of all programs distributed in connection with performances of the Play and in all instances in which the title of the Play appears for purposes of advertising, publicizing or otherwise exploiting the Play and/or a production thereof. The name of the Author must appear on a separate line, in which no other name appears, immediately beneath the title and in size of type equal to 50% of the size of the largest, most prominent letter used for the title of the Play. No person, firm or entity may receive credit larger or more prominent than that accorded the Author.

IPHIGENIA opened at the WorkShop Theater Company (Tony Sportiello, Artistic Director; Riley Jones-Cohen, Executive Director) in New York City, opening on March 22, 2003. It was directed by Elysa Marden; the set design was by Troy Hourie; the costume and mask design were by Isabel Rubio; the lighting design was by Deborah Constantine; the puppet design was by Eric Walton and Michael Lerner; and the stage manager was Rebecca Zuber. The cast was as follows:

AGAMEMNON / MYRMIDON .... Mark Hofmaier
OLD MAN / MYRMIDON .... Katherine Freedman
IPHIGENIA / CALCHAS .... Pauline Tully
MENELAOS / MYRMIDON .... Greg Skura
ODYSSEUS / MESSENGER .... Shamika Cotton
YOUNG WOMAN .... Carrie Edel
CLYTEMNESTRA .... Marinell Madden
ACHILLES .... Brian Christopher Homer

IPHIGENIA was presented in June 2005 at the Samuel Beckett Theatre in the "Sunshine Series" in New York City by Epic Theater Center (Ron Russell and Zak Berkman, Producing Directors). The play was directed by Elysa Marden.

IPHIGENIA was presented in July 2005 by Powerhouse Theatre Company (Beth Fargis-Lancaster, Producing Director) with New York Stage and Film (Elizabeth Timperman, Managing Director) at Vassar College. The play was directed by Emily Mendolsohn.

CHARACTERS

AGAMEMNON — King of Mycenae and commander of the Greek army

MENELAOS — King of Sparta and brother of Agamemnon

IPHIGENIA — the eldest daughter of Agamemnon

CLYTEMNESTRA — Queen of Mycenae and wife of Agamemnon

ACHILLES — commander of the Myrmidons

MYRMIDONS — warriors loyal to Achilles

CALCHAS — a priest

OLD MAN — a servant

YOUNG WOMAN

SOLDIERS

Note on doubling: This play can easily be performed by six actors.

PLACE

The Bay at Aulis in Greece.

TIME

Before the Trojan War.

IPHIGENIA

CHORUS.
Once there were three sisters

Phoebe
Clytemnestra
And Helen
And guess which sister
Everyone wants to marry.

Helen.

So all of the
Fiercest
Biggest
And boldest
Soldiers came from all over Greece
To marry Helen.

"I am here!"
Said the soldier.

"To take your daughter for my queen. My power is large, my purse is great! Take me for your son and give me your daughter."

"Um, hello there,"
Said another.

"I was here first. My country is larger, my power is bigger and
I don't even carry a purse. I have people who do that for me."

"Hold on a moment,"
Said another.

On and on and on they argued over who would get Helen until,

"Pick me or I'll kill him!"

"Pick me or I'll kill myself!"

"Pick me or I'll kill you, him and everyone! Including Helen!"

"Gentlemen please,"
Her good father said.
"Why not swear an oath? You'll have nothing to dread.
Whoever wins Helen shall be protected by all other suitors."

"See, he picked me!"

"I'll kill you!"

"And to be considered as her suitor, you must all swear to protect other suitors in their claim to my daughter, Helen."

Helen!

"Swear."

"We swear!"

"And if any one should carry her off,
Or find his way into her bed,
Or under her pillow, or beneath her silk sheets,
You will kill that man and destroy his city."

"We swear!"

But her father, Tyndareous, relented
And allowed Helen to marry for love.

And she found Menelaos
She married Menelaos
Had children with him
And loved him very much
For a very long time
But that was all a long time ago
A very long time ago

Before Paris came
With golden flowers
And long legs
With slender hands
And long long legs
Those wide shoulders
That delicate mouth
And those long tight handsome legs

He gave her jewels
Her husband was away
He played with her children
Who love him like a father.
Where is their father?
Where did he go?
He's been away a long time.

"Do you think he would mind very much if we took a trip to Troy? To my lands across the sea?"

"But isn't that far?"

"Not so far as all of that. Poor girl, you've not traveled. Why not come then with me and stay for a while? If you really don't like it, you can always return."

So she did
And they left
With the children behind
Alone

And they had a very nice time.

Then Menelaos came home from his journeys and travels
He came home to an empty bed
To his children running wild
Left alone by their mother.

Menelaos came home to no wife

No Helen

And he did not take this well.

"HELEN!"

He went all over Greece for her, looking in vain.

But no one had seen her
For she was off in distant Troy.

He enlisted his brother,
The great King Agamemnon
To lead a great army.

So they rounded up the suitors,
The entire country of Greece
And made them all honor their oaths.

WE HAVE COME HERE TO AULIS
TO GET BACK THE WIFE OF GOOD MENELAOS.

HELEN!
(Singing.)
WE'VE COME TO THE SHORES OF AULIS
TO LAUNCH A THOUSAND SHIPS
WE SAIL ACROSS THE AEGEAN
MAY THE LORD GOD BLESS OUR TRIP

FOR WE'RE FIGHTING FOR OUR FREEDOM
WE'RE FIGHTING FOR OUR PRIDE
THE GREEKS ARRIVE ON YOUR SHORES
TO RETRIEVE OUR NATION'S BRIDE.

THEY STOLE OUR LADY HELEN
THE BLOODY SAVAGES OF TROY
WE WILL NOT REST TIL WE HAVE
THEIR CITY'S WALLS DESTROYED

YES WE'RE FIGHTING FOR OUR FREEDOM
WE'RE FIGHTING FOR OUR PRIDE
THE GREEKS ARRIVE ON YOUR SHORES
WE WON'T LEAVE 'TIL THE TROJANS HAVE DIED!

(The Chorus disperses, leaving Agamemnon alone in very dim light. He is brooding. A twig snaps.)

AGAMEMNON. Who's there?! I heard you, now show yourself!

OLD MAN. It's only me, your majesty. Nobody. *(An old man hobbles toward the stage, with difficulty.)*

AGAMEMNON. I thought I heard something snap.

OLD MAN. My joints, your grace. Not what they used to be.

AGAMEMNON. Nothing is.

OLD MAN. For certain that's the truth. There was a time when I used to be able to remember all of my children's names. And their birthdays no less. Imagine that.

AGAMEMNON. You're one of my wife's servants, aren't you.

OLD MAN. Good of you to remember that, sir, a king such as yourself with all those kingly things on your mind.

AGAMEMNON. Ever thought about it? What it is to be a king?

OLD MAN. Heavens no, sir. I don't have the head for it. Or the stomach. If you'll forgive my saying so.

AGAMEMNON. It does require quite a stomach. *(Pause.)*

OLD MAN. Are you hungry, sir? A bit of venison perhaps. This forest is full of deer. I saw a few soldiers come back last night carrying the biggest buck I have ever seen.

AGAMEMNON. I am only hungry for a home-cooked meal.

OLD MAN. You miss your family then, sir. Well, perhaps you'll see them again soon ...

AGAMEMNON. Why? What have you heard?

OLD MAN. I know nothing. Only I have heard a rumor going 'round that your daughter Iphigenia is to be given up in marriage to the great Achilles. Oh he's a remarkable soldier so they say. Of course we'll see how he fares on the battlefield at Troy, but I imagine he'll hold up pretty well, considering legends —

AGAMEMNON. What else?!

OLD MAN. That she has been sent for to arrive here at Aulis. That's the rumor anyway.

AGAMEMNON. It's not true. I mean it's true, but it isn't.

OLD MAN. Well, sometimes that's how these things work.

AGAMEMNON. You love my family well, don't you?

OLD MAN. More than my own. Of course they're scattered around now, and it is hard to keep up with them. You know I had five daughters at one time …

AGAMEMNON. And you would do anything to keep my family from harm's way.

OLD MAN. I swear I would.

AGAMEMNON. *(Quietly to himself.)* What have I done? What have I done?

OLD MAN. Sir, we've been camped out here in Aulis for months waiting for wind to fill our sails and make for Troy, and this is a lovely spot, mind you, I'm not complaining —

AGAMEMNON. Do I look sane to you?! Would a sane man kill his daughter for a steady breeze?

OLD MAN. No. I don't believe I ever killed any of my daughters —

AGAMEMNON. And yet here I am. And I've sent for my daughter to be married to Achilles.

OLD MAN. So it is true. Oh sir, my heartiest congratulations —

AGAMEMNON. It is all a lie! This whole marriage!

OLD MAN. Now I am confused.

AGAMEMNON. Do you believe in God?

OLD MAN. Oh, yes, sir. Very much.

AGAMEMNON. And if he told you to do something, you'd do it.

OLD MAN. Oh, yes, I think so, sir. Only I don't hear from God all that often.

AGAMEMNON. But if you did, you would do what he said.

OLD MAN. Only I don't hear from him.

AGAMEMNON. If! If you did! If?

OLD MAN. If, then yes.

AGAMEMNON. No matter how terrible it was.

OLD MAN. But how can the will of God be terrible?

AGAMEMNON. Good question! What if he commanded you to sacrifice your daughter?

OLD MAN. But he wouldn't do that.

AGAMEMNON. Oh, yes, he would!

OLD MAN. Why would he do that?

AGAMEMNON. He works in mysterious ways.

OLD MAN. Yes, I've heard that said about him. *(Short pause.)* You see, your majesty … I am not a great man. I try to do my best to honor God as best I can and I don't have a daughter to sacrifice, at least not anymore, I would have to find one and I am not sure that I could, so even if I did find one of them — I don't really hear much from God. I guess he doesn't have much use for me really and who can blame him.

AGAMEMNON. You are lucky, old man.

OLD MAN. Oh very, my lord. I've got a good and just king to serve. What more can any man want?

AGAMEMNON. A fair wind would be nice.

OLD MAN. Yes. It's not much of a wind for sailing, is it. Though it does make for very pleasant swimming.

AGAMEMNON. We cannot go to war with Troy if we can't even get the boats out of the harbor.

OLD MAN. So we're disregarding the poor lady that was abducted by the Trojans then?

AGAMEMNON. Helen! No, we're still going … I just have to do something about the wind.

OLD MAN. Some kind of machine, is it? A contraption with fans then? We're not going to row to Troy, your highness?

AGAMEMNON. No.

OLD MAN. Well, thank God for that.

AGAMEMNON. Yes go ahead and thank him. Praise him! For it is God who has stopped the wind.

OLD MAN. You'll forgive my asking, but did he actually say why?

AGAMEMNON. There was a priest.

OLD MAN. You don't mean Calchas, sir?

AGAMEMNON. Do you know him?

OLD MAN. Only to play cards with. He cheats, you know. *(Calchas and Menelaos appear and the scene flashes back.)*

CALCHAS. King Agamemnon. Hear my words, for they will be grave.

AGAMEMNON. Is it about our war with Troy?

CALCHAS. It is.

AGAMEMNON. We will succeed?

CALCHAS. You may …

MENELAOS. Of course we may, Calchas. What kind of prophecy is that? We may or we may not. He's not a priest, he's a fortune-teller. I say we forget the sails and row.

AGAMEMNON. We cannot simply row all the way to Troy,

Menelaos. For God's sake, let the man speak.

CALCHAS. It is for his sake that I speak. The ships may sail and you will level the barbarous Troy, but he demands a heavy price.

MENELAOS. Whatever the price, we'll pay. I have in my vaults nearly a million pounds of gold —

CALCHAS. Menelaos, this debt belongs to your brother.

AGAMEMNON. To me? What does he want of me?

CALCHAS. Your eldest daughter.

AGAMEMNON. Iphigenia? Truly … *(Calchas nods.)* Then he may have her. All of my children love God well, and if he has some special plans for her then —

CALCHAS. Sir. It's not what you think.

(Crossfade back to scene.)

AGAMEMNON. Calchas said that God was offended, apparently someone killed the wrong deer, and the only way for us to launch the ships was for me to sacrifice my daughter Iphigenia.

OLD MAN. He didn't say that!

AGAMEMNON. Yes, he did, apparently!

OLD MAN. You don't owe that priest any money, do you?

AGAMEMNON. Of course not!

OLD MAN. Wait, you sent for Iphigenia to come to marry Achilles, but it's really to have her killed?!

AGAMEMNON. Keep your voice down.

OLD MAN. But sir, this is horrible!

AGAMEMNON. I know!

OLD MAN. Why, why would you do that?

AGAMEMNON. I DON'T KNOW! I'm trying to follow the will of God.

OLD MAN. You mean the card player.

AGAMEMNON. Look, God wants this war, Greece wants this war, we are going to war! I believed I was being tested.

OLD MAN. But this may only be the word of a card player. Who Cheats. Priests make mistakes.

AGAMEMNON. You may be right. I can't risk it. If it truly is the word of God, then let him show me a sign. I cannot kill my daughter because someone killed the wrong deer!

OLD MAN. Good for you!

AGAMEMNON. I'll write a letter to that effect, telling her not to come.

OLD MAN. So the wedding is canceled?

AGAMEMNON. There never was a wedding!

OLD MAN. Oh, this is all very disappointing! She is a bride to be under false pretenses, only to be killed by her father and then on top of that to have her wedding canceled? Well, she is sure to be one unhappy lady. I can't imagine what her mother will make of all this.
AGAMEMNON. Here it is. Take this to my wife. It tells them the wedding is off and that she mustn't send our daughter to Aulis. Hurry! Do not let my daughter set foot into this camp. Swear!
OLD MAN. I swear I will deliver your letter, my king.
AGAMEMNON. Go now! God forgive me. *(They exit in opposite directions.)*

(Soldiers practice sword-play offstage but within view. One soldier is alone sharpening a blade. A young woman approaches.)
SOLDIER. *(Drawing a blade.)* Who's there? *(The young woman steps forward.)* Oh.
YOUNG WOMAN. Hi.
SOLDIER. Hello.
YOUNG WOMAN. I was just coming down to get some water.
SOLDIER. Help yourself.
YOUNG WOMAN. Didn't mean to frighten you.
SOLDIER. You didn't.
YOUNG WOMAN. I always come down here to wash. Not me, my body. I meant — just to wash my clothes. Because it's a good place for washing.
SOLDIER. Right. You … live around here?
YOUNG WOMAN. Of course. I mean, no. I've been to Aulis before but no, I'm from a little village a few miles from here. It's not far.
SOLDIER. Oh. So you come all the way to Aulis … to do your laundry.
YOUNG WOMAN. Yes, I did. Do. It's my favorite laundry spot.
SOLDIER. Then I'll leave you to it.
YOUNG WOMAN. Oh, but you don't have to go. I mean, you can stay if you want to. There's plenty of — water.
SOLDIER. Yes. It is after all, the sea.
YOUNG WOMAN. So it is.
SOLDIER. Plenty of water for both of us. You wash your linens in saltwater.
YOUNG WOMAN. No better way.
SOLDIER. Does your husband mind it?
YOUNG WOMAN. Oh I'm not married. Still looking for the

right soldier — person. I'm still … I'm just not married yet.
SOLDIER. Well, don't let me prevent you from your chores.
YOUNG WOMAN. Don't let me prevent you from yours. *(He returns to polishing. She tries to wash something but doesn't really have any laundry.)* I'm sorry — is that a sword from Mycenae?
SOLDIER. Why, yes. Yes, it is.
YOUNG WOMAN. I thought so. May I? *(He hands it to her.)* Heavy. Have you ever used it before?
SOLDIER. Of course I have. It's my sword.
YOUNG WOMAN. What was it like, using it?
SOLDIER. Well, it handles well enough, of course it's not my primary weapon which is safe in the family armory —
YOUNG WOMAN. No I mean … what was it like … Using it.
SOLDIER. In battle? *(She nods.)* I'd rather not speak of it on such a lovely day.
YOUNG WOMAN. I saw the princess Iphigenia arrive. You could see them coming for miles up from the hilltop. There must've been a hundred chariots.
SOLDIER. I think there were four.
YOUNG WOMAN. Anyway.
SOLDIER. No, five, if you count the cooking supplies "chariot."
YOUNG WOMAN. May I finish my story please?
SOLDIER. By all means.
YOUNG WOMAN. So there I was watching them come up from under the hill, counting and counting well past five, and then there was this great big splendid one with all kinds of statues on it, dolphins and everything. And I thought this must be the one she's riding in for sure. You should have seen it coming, dazzled my eyes. All covered in jewels.
SOLDIER. Did you see the girl?
YOUNG WOMAN. No. Still, it must have been her chariot, it was so carefully guarded. Have you seen her? They say she's my age. They say she's the most beautiful bride.
SOLDIER. You shouldn't listen to what they have to say.
YOUNG WOMAN. You have seen her then. Oh tell me, what was she like?
SOLDIER. She's short.
YOUNG WOMAN. Oh, she's not as short as all that, is she? I always imagine her as being taller.
SOLDIER. She's short.
YOUNG WOMAN. Shorter than me?

SOLDIER. No. Not that short.

YOUNG WOMAN. What was her face like, was it pale like porcelain? Oh, I knew it would be. And what about her figure, was she …

SOLDIER. She was short! She's too young. *(Short pause.)*

YOUNG WOMAN. I didn't mean to …

SOLDIER. No, I apologize. You must forgive me.

YOUNG WOMAN. What is she too young for? *(Suddenly the soldiers rush off toward something offstage, speaking incoherently but with much enthusiasm. The soldier stands up and leaves the young woman behind. She exits.)*

MENELAOS. *(Offstage, roaring.)* Agamemnon! *(The lights shift harshly. Menelaos enters with the letter, the old man following desperately.)* Agamemnon!

OLD MAN. My king! My lord!

MENELAOS. Get away, you idiot.

OLD MAN. I have to deliver that letter. I swore I would do it, and I'm good for my word.

MENELAOS. Then you've sworn an oath of treason.

OLD MAN. Nevertheless, an oath is an oath sir, and I'm good for my word.

MENELAOS. You love your master too well.

OLD MAN. Thank you, sir.

MENELAOS. You'll die for your master if you don't keep your peace.

OLD MAN. How can I keep at peace if I don't keep my word?

MENELAOS. Enough with your word. AGAMEMNON! *(Agamemnon enters.)*

AGAMEMNON. Menelaos, what's the problem?

MENELAOS. This! And you!

AGAMEMNON. So now you're going through my mail?

MENELAOS. To stop a treason, yes, I opened your mail.

AGAMEMNON. Treason is a large word for someone who would risk the life of every Greek because he cannot keep track of his wife.

MENELAOS. That's all this war is about to you?

AGAMEMNON. Your wife ran off with another man, Menelaos. My daughter had nothing to do with it!

MENELAOS. You are blind.

AGAMEMNON. No, I finally see. You have become a greedy man.

MENELAOS. I'm not the one who had to command the Greek army. Who had to launch a thousand ships. Don't pretend you didn't want that, you've already commissioned a statue of it! So don't try and tell me it was all about Helen.

AGAMEMNON. If she didn't run off —

MENELAOS. She was abducted!

AGAMEMNON. Then we wouldn't be here!

MENELAOS. Wouldn't we? You don't think we would have found some other reason to go to war? Some insult, trade problems, the will of God, what's the difference. Let's face it. We're Greeks. Every twenty or thirty years, we are going to go to war. And here our cause is just. "Greece is an idea. It means nothing if it doesn't protect its people." That's what you said. And you were right. Remember, Troy started this war, not us. You brought us here, you're our commander. Lead us. Don't be afraid to be who you are. There's no shame in that.

AGAMEMNON. I should feel no shame when I cut my daughter's throat. *(Pause.)* I told her she was getting married. To Achilles. I had to think of something to tell my wife. When a man asks for his wife to send his daughter, his virgin daughter, to a camp with ten thousand soldiers, she wants a reason. She thinks she is getting married. She must be dreaming about him and their life together in … well wherever he lives. Having children together, falling in love if they're lucky, taking walks in an olive grove and all of that. Perhaps she's worrying about that first night. Anticipating it, fearing it. She's not thinking that her father is going to kill her. No love, no children, no olive grove. And why? Because her uncle cannot keep track of her good Aunt Helen. And there is no shame in that, right? Shame is all that I am going to have left. *(Shouts and cheers from offstage.)*

MENELAOS. These are not the words of a general.

AGAMEMNON. Just a father.

MENELAOS. But you are greater than that. Anyone can be a father. The army's full of fathers. But who can inspire these men and lead them on to victory? You.

(Enter the old man.)

OLD MAN. My lord.

AGAMEMNON. They're here?

OLD MAN. Your wife, the lady Clytemnestra, is here and she has … people with her. Many people, sir. I'm afraid it caused quite a stir at the edge of town.

AGAMEMNON. And my daughter?

OLD MAN. She is here, sir. She still imagines that she is getting married. She seemed most enthusiastic about the upcoming nuptials. I hadn't the heart to look at her. But many did.

AGAMEMNON. The soldiers.

OLD MAN. They were waiting to welcome the girl with wreaths and garlands, which apparently they often do in honor of a sacrifice. Only the girl didn't know that, and she put them on and began dancing around in celebration of the wedding.

AGAMEMNON. Enough.

OLD MAN. I failed you and the girl. I'll go now and let you figure this out. *(The old man leaves.)*

AGAMEMNON. She's here. And the soldiers have seen her. It's too late. My little girl has come. Of course she's come, I told her to. Could you do this to your little girl? *(Handing him a knife.)* I'm asking. *(Pause.)*

MENELAOS. I don't know. I'm not the king. Question is, can you do it? *(He hands him back the knife.)*

AGAMEMNON. Do I have a choice?

MENELAOS. You made your choice when you swore to uphold our oaths and lead this army to victory.

AGAMEMNON. Then I shall resign!

MENELAOS. You can't.

AGAMEMNON. Who will stop me?! Who will dare stand between me and my family? *(Short pause.)*

MENELAOS. Greece.

IPHIGENIA. DADDY! *(Iphigenia runs to her father. She wears a garland.)*

AGAMEMNON. Iphigenia.

IPHIGENIA. Daddy! *(They embrace.)*

AGAMEMNON. Oh … What a sight you are.

IPHIGENIA. Please, I look terrible. It was such a long journey with no place to bathe or wash your hair. And so dusty. No one mentioned all the dust. But then you look well! All decked out in your soldier's uniform. You cut an imposing figure, Father. You'll scare them to death, all of those godless barbarian Trojans! Don't you think so, Uncle?

MENELAOS. I'm sure of it.

IPHIGENIA. Good to see you, Uncle. *(Kisses him.)* Yuck. Stubble. Please make this general shave, Father.

AGAMEMNON. Yes …

IPHIGENIA. Did you hear the big news?

MENELAOS. What news?

IPHIGENIA. I'M GETTING MARRIED! To a superstar! Do you know him? Is he as great as everyone says he is? Well he couldn't be, but even if he's half that, I'll count myself lucky. Is cousin Hermione here? I was hoping she could help me with my wedding gown.

MENELAOS. What? No. I'm sorry. She's at home.

IPHIGENIA. You miss her then.

MENELAOS. My daughter? Yes, of course I miss her.

IPHIGENIA. You were thinking of Aunt Helen. It's all right, Uncle. I'd miss her too. She's so beautiful. Hermione and I used to sneak into her dressing room to watch her dress. Not to see her naked or anything like that. Gross. Just to watch her put on clothes and apply her oils. To comb her hair. But don't worry, Uncle, Father will save her. God, I love Aulis! It's so pretty here. Maybe we should all stay here together. You missed me, didn't you? Bet you missed me more than Mother. She's always getting at him. Who do you miss more, Cousin Hermione or Aunt Helen?

AGAMEMNON. *(Too loudly.)* That's enough!

IPHIGENIA. What? I'm just playing.

AGAMEMNON. These aren't the things to play with.

IPHIGENIA. You're right, Father, I'm sorry. Sorry, Uncle. Of course you must miss them both equally. *(Short pause.)* Tell you what. I'm going to cancel the war.

AGAMEMNON. You're what?

IPHIGENIA. Hear ye, hear ye! The war on Troy has officially been canceled!

MENELAOS. *(Interrupting.)* Why don't we —

AGAMEMNON. That's enough.

IPHIGENIA. Go back to your wives and children!

AGAMEMNON. Stop it!

CLYTEMNESTRA. I think it's a fine idea. *(Clytemnestra has entered.)*

IPHIGENIA. I was just telling Father that I've decided to cancel the war on Troy, in honor of my wedding day.

CLYTEMNESTRA. Good for you. Hello.

AGAMEMNON. Hello. Why have you come?

CLYTEMNESTRA. "Iphigenia, apparently you are to be married to the world famous Achilles. Congratulations."

IPHIGENIA. "Thank you very much!"

CLYTEMNESTRA. "Now, go off into the desert, cross it alone and have a nice life."

IPHIGENIA. "But aren't you coming, Mother?"

CLYTEMNESTRA. "No thanks, I'm busy with the wash."

AGAMEMNON. It is a long journey.

CLYTEMNESTRA. Yes, it was. And dusty too. Did you know it would be that dusty?

IPHIGENIA. I told him.

CLYTEMNESTRA. They don't tell you about the dust. But to see you again, makes it all quite worth it.

IPHIGENIA. Aren't you going to kiss her?

MENELAOS. *(To Agamemnon.)* We will speak further. *(To Iphigenia.)* Come, let me show you to your tent. Your parents have much to discuss.

IPHIGENIA. They haven't seen each other in months, I bet they leave the discussion for afterwards. What? I know about men and women and what goes on. I'm all grown up, and I am getting married! Did you hear, Uncle? *(Smug.)* I'm getting married.

CLYTEMNESTRA. Go on now, dear.

IPHIGENIA. Can I get a bath?

MENELAOS. Of course.

IPHIGENIA. No peeking!

MENELAOS. *(Trifle embarrassed.)* Of course not. *(Menelaos and Iphigenia exit.)*

CLYTEMNESTRA. No kiss? *(He kisses her.)* You don't like surprises, I know, I'm sorry, I was just so excited. And I wanted to see you. So tell me about this Achilles.

AGAMEMNON. You've never heard of him?

CLYTEMNESTRA. Stories, sure. But I want to hear it from you. Why did you select him for our daughter?

AGAMEMNON. He is a mighty soldier, and he's a loyal man.

CLYTEMNESTRA. *(Playfully.)* Will he be as kind to her as you have been to me?

AGAMEMNON. Don't start that up again.

CLYTEMNESTRA. I wasn't referring to that —

AGAMEMNON. It was ages ago and before I knew you.

CLYTEMNESTRA. Seems like yesterday you killed my baby and my husband.

AGAMEMNON. It was a war!

CLYTEMNESTRA. It was in my bedroom!

AGAMEMNON. When are you going to put the past behind us?!

CLYTEMNESTRA. Isn't this a war? Aren't you going to war?

AGAMEMNON. God willing.

CLYTEMNESTRA. Menelaos willing, you mean. Yes, that's what you men do, you go to war. For the will of God. Or the will of Menelaos. Or the will of the wind.
AGAMEMNON. What did you say?
CLYTEMNESTRA. The will of the wind.
AGAMEMNON. What made you say that? Tell me!
CLYTEMNESTRA. Nothing. I only meant that you soldiers go to war wherever the wind takes you. And you have no wind to take you this time. It was a play on words. What's eating you? *(She embraces him.)* It's Iphigenia, isn't it? You're worried about her future.
AGAMEMNON. I am.
CLYTEMNESTRA. They grow up so fast. You feel certain about this Achilles, don't you? Then I do too. I'm sure he will make her happy.
AGAMEMNON. When we get back from Troy.
CLYTEMNESTRA. There's not going to be a honeymoon? What kind of father are you? You marry off our daughter to a total stranger, and then you whisk the groom off halfway across the world, leaving her alone with no honeymoon?
AGAMEMNON. He will protect her.
CLYTEMNESTRA. He's off in Troy with you! And Helen!
AGAMEMNON. He's a great warrior. We need him to win the war. Try and understand that.
CLYTEMNESTRA. I don't understand.
AGAMEMNON. Then please. Leave everything to me. *(Pause.)*
CLYTEMNESTRA. Protect her from whom?
AGAMEMNON. What?
CLYTEMNESTRA. You said he would protect her. From whom? Why does she need protection?
AGAMEMNON. She doesn't.
CLYTEMNESTRA. Then why did you say that? Your face is turning red. *(Short pause.)* What are you hiding? Don't protect me from the truth. You know how I hate that and I'll know. And then you'll know I know you're lying. It could begin to get under my skin.
AGAMEMNON. You are a treacherous woman.
CLYTEMNESTRA. *(Coyly.)* I try not to be.
AGAMEMNON. I am happy to see you. *(They cuddle again, a bit sexually.)*
CLYTEMNESTRA. Yes, I see that in your cheery demeanor.
AGAMEMNON. I have a lot on my mind.
CLYTEMNESTRA. I know. Let me help you relax …

AGAMEMNON. There is something you can do.
CLYTEMNESTRA. *(Kissing his ear and touching him.)* Ahhh, tell me.
AGAMEMNON. Tomorrow morning.
CLYTEMNESTRA. But what about tonight?
AGAMEMNON. Tomorrow morning, I want you to go home.
CLYTEMNESTRA. What?!
AGAMEMNON. I will see our daughter safely married.
CLYTEMNESTRA. I am the mother of the bride and I have a right to be here at her wedding. Besides, who's going to organize the whole thing, we have to plan the banquet —
AGAMEMNON. It's not safe for you to be here amongst all of these soldiers.
CLYTEMNESTRA. You don't trust your own army? They must be great men indeed if the king and commander cannot trust his own soldiers with the safety of his wife. How do you think they'll like my sister?
AGAMEMNON. I hope they like her as well as she deserves. *(They exit.)*

(Crossfade to the Myrmidons' camp. The Myrmidons are depicted by three hand puppets.)
MYRMIDON 1. I hate Trojans.
MYRMIDON 2. I hate Troy.
MYRMIDON 1. Yes. Troy is the worst!
MYRMIDON 2. It stinks.
MYRMIDON 1. It smells.
MYRMIDON 2. And it's full of Trojans.
MYRMIDON 1. I hate Trojans.
MYRMIDON 3. Do you know any Trojans?
MYRMIDON 1. No.
MYRMIDON 2. What's it to you?
MYRMIDON 3. Not a thing. I'm just curious. Have you ever met any Trojans?
MYRMIDON 1. Hell no. We hate the Trojans! We're the Myrmidons and we fight with Achilles!
MYRMIDON 2. Yeah, what do we want with a bunch of Trojans? We hate Trojans!
MYRMIDON 1. And Troy!
MYRMIDON 2. You're not a Trojan by any chance?
MYRMIDON 3. Why do you ask?

MYRMIDON 2. You seem to know all about Trojans.
MYRMIDON 3. Not a bit. I've never met one. And I am a true Myrmidon through and through. In fact, I can safely say that I believe I have never set eyes on a Trojan in the whole of my life.
MYRMIDON 1. Nor I!
MYRMIDON 2. Nor I!
MYRMIDON 3. Which is why I have no opinion of them whatsoever. *(They are confused.)* Although I suspect we'll all be meeting plenty of Trojans in the not-too-distant future.
MYRMIDON 1. What is this?!
MYRMIDON 2. What do you mean?
MYRMIDON 1. Speak up!
MYRMIDON 2. Explain yourself!
MYRMIDON 3. We are after all going to war with Troy.
MYRMIDON 1. So?
MYRMIDON 2. And?
MYRMIDON 3. Well, I imagine that Troy is likely to be filled with a bunch of Trojans.
MYRMIDON 1. I hate Trojans.
(Achilles enters and addresses his puppet warriors.)
ACHILLES. Then you're in luck because we won't be sailing today.
MYRMIDON 3. No wind again.
ACHILLES. Not a bit. And there doesn't seem to be any sign of any change. Menelaos wants us all to row these boats across the sea.
MYRMIDON 1. I hate rowing to Troy!
MYRMIDON 3. Isn't it rather far, Achilles?
ACHILLES. We could make it, God willing.
MYRMIDON 3. Perhaps it's not in the cards for us to go to Troy.
ACHILLES. No, it's in the cards all right. We swore an oath, as Myrmidons and as Greeks we will vanquish the foes of our friends and conquer the Trojan barbarians and rescue the lady Helen.
MYRMIDON 2. Who's Helen?
ACHILLES. Don't you men listen? Helen is the whole reason we are going. The barbarian Paris has abducted Helen the most beautiful woman of all of Greece, and taken her to the land of Troy.
(The Myrmidons are shocked.)
MYRMIDON 3. That's outrageous!
ACHILLES. If we don't stop them now, then what's to stop them from taking all of our women?
MYRMIDON 3. Maybe we should go back to our own land and protect our women.

MYRMIDON 2. Yes, let's go home! Screw Helen!
MYRMIDON 1. Let's screw Helen!
ACHILLES. Nobody is screwing Helen.
MYRMIDON 2. Why not?
ACHILLES. Because we're trying to save her!
MYRMIDONS. Oh! / I get it. / This is very confusing. / Save Helen, don't kill her.
ACHILLES. I'm going to meet with Agamemnon and see what his plan is. Let's get this war on the road! Who's with me?!
MYRMIDON 3. What should we do?
ACHILLES. Just — try and stay in shape, fellows, all right? Don't eat too much venison. After all, you're the mighty Myrmidons! You're the —
ALL. Mighty Myrmidons! Yaaaay! *(Achilles runs out slapping the Myrmidons in the head as he goes.)*
MYRMIDON 3. He sometimes lays it on a bit thick, doesn't he. *(They exit.)*

(The young woman holds the blade while a soldier folds some clothing.)
YOUNG WOMAN. I've never killed a man before. I've tried a couple of times, but it didn't work out. Just haven't found the right guy, I guess.
SOLDIER. Have you tried poison?
YOUNG WOMAN. It's not the same.
SOLDIER. No.
YOUNG WOMAN. So have you done it? Killed people.
SOLDIER. I'm a soldier and I'm alive.
YOUNG WOMAN. Did you know any of them?
SOLDIER. Of course not. They were the enemy.
YOUNG WOMAN. Anyone can kill the enemy. I think I'd rather kill a nice man, an innocent man. You know — someone who plants flowers and bows to ladies in the marketplace.
SOLDIER. *(Bowing to her.)* Like this.
YOUNG WOMAN. Just like that. Someone who plays with his children and kisses his mother on his birthday. I want to kill that man.
SOLDIER. Now why would that be?
YOUNG WOMAN. No reason. Why does everyone feel like they had to come up with some bogus reason behind every person they kill? God doesn't use reasons, that's for sure.
SOLDIER. You don't think he has a plan for us.
YOUNG WOMAN. Look around you. One day, a perfectly nice

family sits down to dinner in their nice little house by their little river. They all bow their heads and say their little prayers giving thanks for the bread and hopes for the future and they're all so happy to be this happy together and they only wish that it could go on forever 'til death do us part when all of a sudden a boulder falls on the house and kills everyone in the room! Splat! Why? No reason. God just felt like rolling a boulder.

SOLDIER. But perhaps someone in this family did something wrong and they are being punished for it.

YOUNG WOMAN. If you die in Troy, will they say he had it coming?

SOLDIER. I hope not.

YOUNG WOMAN. But you've killed people.

SOLDIER. In defense of my country.

YOUNG WOMAN. Well, wouldn't the dead guy say the same thing?

SOLDIER. Perhaps.

YOUNG WOMAN. So I think God looks down at everybody on the ground and sees a mass of people just killing each other in defense of their country, and he decides to roll a boulder. And there's nothing anyone can do about it.

(Iphigenia is fixing her hair. Clytemnestra enters.)

IPHIGENIA. Mother, will you help me with my hair? I can't seem to get it to fall right and it has to be perfect.

CLYTEMNESTRA. It will be. You have such fine hair, it's always been difficult.

IPHIGENIA. Oh God, why am I so nervous?

CLYTEMNESTRA. Of course you're nervous. I was. On the night of my wedding to your father, I kept thinking … am I supposed to do something or am I supposed to just wait for him. Know what I mean?

IPHIGENIA. Yes.

CLYTEMNESTRA. I couldn't decide if I should get undressed, or would that be too presumptuous. And I was so nervous that when he opened the door and pulled back the curtains I practically —

IPHIGENIA. Mother, stop!

CLYTEMNESTRA. What?

IPHIGENIA. Enough. I don't want to hear about you and Daddy.

CLYTEMNESTRA. Why not?

IPHIGENIA. Because then on my night I'm going to be lying

there thinking of you two which is just … let's not go there.
CLYTEMNESTRA. I thought you'd be curious.
IPHIGENIA. I am. I will be. It's just — I'm fine. I know everything I need to know. Let's just do the hair.
CLYTEMNESTRA. You're sure.
IPHIGENIA. Yeah.
CLYTEMNESTRA. You haven't already …
IPHIGENIA. Mother, you're supposed to be helping me to relax, so quit pestering me. Sorry. It's just that everything's fine in that department. At least, I think it will be. I hope so anyway. I'm sorry, I know you're trying to help, it just makes me tense, so let's just talk about something else.
CLYTEMNESTRA. All right.
IPHIGENIA. For instance, this war. I've been looking at some maps and they've got Troy written down all over the place. Nobody knows exactly where it is. Sometimes it's drawn on an island, sometimes it's surrounded by mountains. So the first thing we have to do is even find Troy.
CLYTEMNESTRA. Honey.
IPHIGENIA. Then we've got another serious problem. I read that Troy is fortified with these giant stone walls which are apparently more than twelve feet thick. Twelve feet. Do you know what that means?
CLYTEMNESTRA. I need to tell you something.
IPHIGENIA. It means that if we try and drill a hole through those walls, say at least six by six in order to be wide enough to get a few men through it at the same time, I estimate we're going to be at it for at least seventy-two hours straight if everything goes well and that's not even taking into account that they're going to be hurling down rocks and boulders at us from high atop the city walls. Not going to be easy.
CLYTEMNESTRA. You do realize you're not going to Troy.
IPHIGENIA. What? Why? You knew?
CLYTEMNESTRA. Your father just told me.
IPHIGENIA. But he needs Achilles to win this war and if I am to be married to him tomorrow then I have to go to Troy, right?
CLYTEMNESTRA. Apparently not.
IPHIGENIA. That doesn't make any sense. What — am I supposed to get married and then — what?
CLYTEMNESTRA. I want you to come home with me.
IPHIGENIA. Great. No offense. But I'm an adult. I'm getting

married. And I don't want to go home with my mother. *(Achilles can be heard, off.)*
ACHILLES. Where is the general of the Greek army?! It is I, Achilles!
IPHIGENIA. It's him! I'm not ready.
CLYTEMNESTRA. Go inside. I'll deal with him. *(Iphigenia exits as Achilles enters.)*
ACHILLES. Agamemnon!
CLYTEMNESTRA. Well, hello, young man.
ACHILLES. A woman? And a beautiful one too.
CLYTEMNESTRA. Wait until you meet my daughter.
ACHILLES. TWO women! These are strange times. My lady, I cannot be seen alone with two women. That would be … illegal.
CLYTEMNESTRA. Please, I must speak to you.
ACHILLES. To me? Why?
CLYTEMNESTRA. I am Clytemnestra, Queen of Mycenae, wife of Agamemnon. Iphigenia's mother. Helen's sister? Does any of this sound familiar?
ACHILLES. Of course, lady, you're the queen. I beg your pardon. I don't mean to intrude, I was looking for your husband.
CLYTEMNESTRA. Well, he's not here right now.
ACHILLES. Right. OK. Well, I'll check back later then.
CLYTEMNESTRA. I think you should stay. After all, you've never met my daughter.
ACHILLES. I'm sure she's a lovely girl.
CLYTEMNESTRA. Oh, she's a full-grown woman.
ACHILLES. Take your word for it.
CLYTEMNESTRA. Don't you want to meet her?
ACHILLES. Frankly, no.
CLYTEMNESTRA. You're not the least bit curious.
ACHILLES. You've seen one, you've seen them all.
CLYTEMNESTRA. Well, where I come from a woman only has one husband.
ACHILLES. I believe in that.
CLYTEMNESTRA. Unless, of course, in my case, where I start with one husband and then another man comes along and murders the first one before taking me for a wife.
ACHILLES. Yes, well, there can be extenuating circumstances.
CLYTEMNESTRA. You don't want to meet your future wife?
ACHILLES. Oh, yes, I do. Just not until the future when I meet my wife.
CLYTEMNESTRA. But now it's time to meet her.

ACHILLES. It is?

CLYTEMNESTRA. So I've been led to believe.

ACHILLES. Do you know who it is?

CLYTEMNESTRA. My daughter. Iphigenia.

ACHILLES. I am supposed to marry your daughter?

CLYTEMNESTRA. Well, aren't you?

ACHILLES. Am I?

CLYTEMNESTRA. Achilles!

ACHILLES. I'm sorry, I don't know what to say.

CLYTEMNESTRA. Then it's not true.

ACHILLES. Well, it's the first I've heard of it. I think. No, definitely. They told me to bring my army, the mighty Myrmidons, here to Aulis to join the Greek army to attack Troy and retrieve the virtuous Helen.

CLYTEMNESTRA. And that's all.

ACHILLES. Yes.

CLYTEMNESTRA. Nothing about …

ACHILLES. Oh, and that I should be careful of my heel.

CLYTEMNESTRA. Your heel?

ACHILLES. It doesn't really bother me, but there are these rumors that my mother dipped me …

CLYTEMNESTRA. Nothing about my daughter.

ACHILLES. Nothing. I'm sorry.

CLYTEMNESTRA. I am going to kill my husband.

ACHILLES. Oh I wish you wouldn't. See, I am sworn to protect him too, so it would really put me in an awkward position.

OLD MAN. My queen, I must speak with you! *(The old man enters.)* You have been deceived, there is to be no wedding.

CLYTEMNESTRA. We know that.

OLD MAN. Agamemnon sent word for the young girl to come to Aulis under the false pretense that she should be married.

CLYTEMNESTRA. Then what is the true purpose?

OLD MAN. O lady. The seas have calmed here at Aulis. The priest says that he has heard a word from God that in order for the winds to blow … your daughter is to be sacrificed. *(Pause.)*

CLYTEMNESTRA. He did not do this.

OLD MAN. He made a terrible mistake. He had a change in heart. He ordered me to come back to you in Argos to stop her from coming.

CLYTEMNESTRA. Then WHY DIDN'T YOU STOP ME?!

OLD MAN. I tried. I was too late. Menelaos delayed me. I am so sorry, lady.

CLYTEMNESTRA. *(To herself.)* Don't panic. I've got to think, there's still time. There must be something I can do …

ACHILLES. I hate that they used my name!

CLYTEMNESTRA. Achilles, you must help us. My daughter was said to be your wife. She deserves your protection.

ACHILLES. Count on it. No harm will come to her. I have the mighty Myrmidons at my beck and call. *(They exit.)*

(The Myrmidons try to work out the song, using the same melody from the beginning. Myrmidon 3 is conducting.)

MYRMIDONS.
    WE'RE OFF TO KILL THE TROJANS
    TO RECLAIM ACHILLES' BRIDE.

MYRMIDON 3. Wait a minute. Point of order here. Achilles isn't married.

MYRMIDON 1. So?

MYRMIDON 2. And?

MYRMIDON 3. So why are we reclaiming his bride?

MYRMIDONS. Hmm. / That's a tough one. / Whose bride is it we're meant to save?
    WE'RE OFF TO KILL THE SPARTANS / TROJANS
    TO RECLAIM AN IMPORTANT BRIDE.

MYRMIDON 3. No, not kill the Spartans.

MYRMIDON 1. I hate Spartans.

MYRMIDON 3. You used to hate Spartans, but now they are our friends. Because we're all on the same team.

MYRMIDON 2. That's stupid.

MYRMIDON 1. Yeah, we hate the Spartans.

MYRMIDON 2. Spartans are Mean.

MYRMIDON 3. Not anymore. Spartans are our allies in the coalition.

MYRMIDON 1. Oh.

MYRMIDON 2. What's a coalition?

MYRMIDON 3. *(Reciting from school.)* A coalition is a group of armies who join together to fight a common enemy.

MYRMIDON 2. The Athenians!

MYRMIDON 1. Yes!

MYRMIDON 3. No.

MYRMIDON 2. Athenians are worse than the Spartans.

MYRMIDON 1. Die, Athenian, die!

MYRMIDONS 1 and 2. *(Making up lyrics as they go along.)*
    WE'RE OFF TO KILL ATHENIANS
    BECAUSE THEY'RE REALLY MEAN
MYRMIDON 2.
    THEY'RE EVEN WORSE THAN SPARTANS
MYRMIDON 1.
    THEY'RE REALLY REALLY MEAN
MYRMIDON 2. No no,
    LET'S STICK THEM IN THE LATRINE.
MYRMIDON 1. Yeah, that's a good one! Let's stick them in the latrine!
MYRMIDON 3. Are you quite through?
MYRMIDONS 1 and 2.
    WE'RE OFF TO KILL THE SPARTANS
    BECAUSE THEY'RE REALLY MEAN
    THEY'RE EVEN WORSE THAN ATHENIANS
    LET'S STICK THEM IN THE LATRINE!
MYRMIDON 3. The Spartans are our friends! The Athenians are our friends!
MYRMIDON 1. I hate our friends.
MYRMIDON 3. They're all key members of our coalition.
MYRMIDON 2. Whose side are you on?
MYRMIDON 1. Yeah!
MYRMIDON 3. I'm on your side, everyone's on your side. They are all your friends.
MYRMIDON 2. If everyone is our friend, who are we supposed to kill?
MYRMIDON 3. The enemy?
MYRMIDONS 1 and 2. The enemy!
MYRMIDON 1. Let's kill the enemy.
MYRMIDONS.
    WE'RE OFF TO KILL THE ENEMY.
    TO KILL SOMEONE ELSE'S / MENELAOS' BRIDE …
MYRMIDON 3. No, that's still wrong. It goes,
    WE'RE OFF TO KILL THE … SOMEONE …
    WE'RE OFF TO KILL THE ENEMY …
    WE'RE OFF TO KILL THE …
MYRMIDON 2. Who was the enemy again?
MYRMIDON 3. I had it a minute ago. It's on the tip of my tongue. Oh hang it all.
MYRMIDON 1. Maybe the enemy is our friend.

(The young woman approaches the soldier near the camp. Other soldiers are nearby, restless.)
YOUNG WOMAN. They are actually going to kill her!
SOLDIER. Keep your voice down. *(He takes her aside.)*
YOUNG WOMAN. Does she know? Has anyone thought to tell her?
SOLDIER. I honestly don't know.
YOUNG WOMAN. How can this be happening?
SOLDIER. There was a prophecy.
YOUNG WOMAN. So, whatever God says to do, it's all right.
SOLDIER. It's not that simple.
YOUNG WOMAN. These people who claim, "God told them to do it." You ever seen these people up close? They're kind of terrifying, the way they look at you like they just ate a live pigeon. "God told me to kill my daughter! God has sent me to kill the infidels!" It's never anything like, "God demands that I plant a vegetable garden! Or build a school or a hospital!" It's always how he wants you to slaughter the firstborn sons of everybody. Are you sure you heard that right? Are you sure it wasn't, "God wants me to be locked up somewhere in a deep, deep hole." I don't know, maybe I'd feel different if I actually heard God talk. Face to face, you know? But I'm glad I don't if this is the stuff he says. So what are you going to do about it?
SOLDIER. What do you want me to do?
YOUNG WOMAN. Save her! Stop it from happening!
SOLDIER. Why are you taking this so personally?
YOUNG WOMAN. Why aren't you?
SOLDIER. It's not my choice.
YOUNG WOMAN. So if you and I were married and we had a baby girl of our own and some priest told you to sacrifice her to get some better sailing weather, what are you going to do about it?
SOLDIER. It doesn't matter what I'd do about it —
YOUNG WOMAN. *(Over his lines.)* Matters to me!
SOLDIER. It's not my decision!
YOUNG WOMAN. So make it yours! Stand up for something.
SOLDIER. It's not my choice! I'm not the king. I'm a soldier. I go where they point me. I don't make decisions about when to go to war. I kill people. Good people, bad people — that's for kings to decide. I kill who they put in front of me, all right?! *(Pause.)* Look, when you're out there on the battlefield … usually there's some kid next to you. Scared, little shaky. Got to know him on the boat

coming over. Where he's from, things he likes. Maybe he's got this little baby girl he won't shut up about. She's only one year old and she's just starting to stand up, take hold of things. And he goes on and on all night long about how her teeth are coming in, just peeking through the gums. They're probably already in by now, but when he left they were just popping out — these little tiny pearly white teeth. She's teething right, it's keeping them up nights so he goes over to the baby while his wife is asleep and he puts a single grape in the palm of his hand and crushes it with his pinky, so the juice falls out onto his finger. Then he sticks his pinky into his little girl's mouth. And he rubs her gums and her tiny new teeth. That guy. That's why you fight a war. *(Four other soldiers appear.)*
SOLDIER 3. Have you heard anything?
SOLDIER. Nothing.
SOLDIER 3. There's a delay.
SOLDIER 2. The king.
SOLDIER 4. He's weak.
SOLDIER 5. He's vexed. Who wouldn't be?
SOLDIER 2. We should do the girl ourselves.
SOLDIER 5. Do what to her?
SOLDIER. The prophecy says it has to be the father.
SOLDIER 3. Agamemnon may not be up to the task.
SOLDIER 2. Who can blame him?
SOLDIER. He'll come through.
SOLDIER 2. They say he's frightened of his wife.
SOLDIER 4. You would be too.
SOLDIER 5. Seriously, this isn't funny. She's going to be heartbroken.
SOLDIER 4. What do you care?
YOUNG WOMAN. Perhaps he's had a change of heart.
SOLDIER 3. Who is this?
SOLDIER. She's with me.
SOLDIER 3. She knows something.
SOLDIER 2. Look at her.
SOLDIER 4. I like her.
SOLDIER 5. Come on, guys.
SOLDIER 3. Tell me, dear, are you with the king's family?
SOLDIER. Leave her.
SOLDIER 3. She's hiding something.
SOLDIER 2. Look at her!
SOLDIER 4. She looks good.

SOLDIER 5. Maybe we should get back to camp.
SOLDIER. She's with me.
SOLDIER 3. Is she now?
SOLDIER 2. Wanna bet?
SOLDIER 5. We're going to get into trouble.
SOLDIER 3. When did all this come about?
SOLDIER. Let me take you home.
SOLDIER 4. Hold on a minute. Let someone else have a chance.
SOLDIER 2. Hi. How are you?
SOLDIER 5. They don't mean any harm really, it's just they haven't seen a woman in a long time.
SOLDIER 4. Why don't you go pitch a tent?
SOLDIER 3. Let's hear what the girl has to say.
SOLDIER. She has nothing to say.
YOUNG WOMAN. Yes, I do. No real king would ever hurt his own children for any reason. And if Agamemnon is a true king, then he'll see that and send her home.
SOLDIER 3. So you would like to see this girl escape?
YOUNG WOMAN. I would.
SOLDIER. Don't.
SOLDIER 2. Feisty!
SOLDIER 4. We've caught a live one!
SOLDIER 5. That's a perfectly naturally reaction. No one wants to see anyone hurt.
SOLDIER 3. Would you help her do it?
YOUNG WOMAN. If it would save her from the likes of you.
SOLDIER. She doesn't know what she's saying.
YOUNG WOMAN. Yes I do.
SOLDIER 3. Take her.
SOLDIER 2. No problem!
SOLDIER 4. She's mine.
SOLDIER 5. Careful!
SOLDIER. *(Drawing swords.)* Do not touch her.
YOUNG WOMAN. Let me go …
SOLDIER 3. She would inform the princess. That's treason. She said so herself.
SOLDIER 5. I don't know if that's technically treason.
SOLDIER. I'll look after her.
SOLDIER 3. Come.
SOLDIER 2. Come with us!
SOLDIER 4. No, come with me.

SOLDIER 5. Maybe I should see her safely home.
YOUNG WOMAN. You're hurting me.
SOLDIER. Do not touch her. Don't make me say it again.
SOLDIER 2. Look at this one!
SOLDIER 4. "Do not touch her!"
SOLDIER 3. Put up your swords.
SOLDIER 2. No, I'll handle him. Haven't tasted any blood in a long time.
SOLDIER 5. That's disgusting.
SOLDIER 3. Think what you're doing. This girl is a traitor. She's confessed as much. She would inform the girl against our king's command.
SOLDIER. I will handle her myself. *(She pulls out a knife.)*
YOUNG WOMAN. You? None of you will handle me.
SOLDIER 3. Don't let her get away!
SOLDIER. Come back! *(She runs. They chase her.)*
SOLDIER 5. So much violence.

(Crossfade to another camp where Achilles, Menelaos, Agamemnon and Calchas pace and wait in the dark.)
MENELAOS. We can't wait any longer for the wind! The men have grown restless. They've seen the girl and if we don't act now, there will be violence among our soldiers, I'm telling you.
ACHILLES. We can't control our own men? We haven't even started yet!
MENELAOS. You cannot wait.
ACHILLES. Dismiss the army. They're worthless anyway.
MENELAOS. There's a rumor that if you don't act, they'll kill the girl themselves.
CALCHAS. No. It must be a holy sacrifice. You must do this. Great Achilles, you must fight with us. It is the will of God.
ACHILLES. I came here of my own free will! What's holy about any of this? Somebody tell me. You want war and I'll give you a war but it was my name they used. My name, Achilles, that brought this girl. And my name will not be used so lightly.
AGAMEMNON. Take it back then. Take the Myrmidons back. Go on. Get out of here. We'll make this war without your help.
ACHILLES. Is that so?
AGAMEMNON. You heard me. Go.
ACHILLES. Good. I'm through with this.
CALCHAS. He cannot leave.

ACHILLES. Try and stop me.

CALCHAS. The prophecy says that Achilles shall strike down the walls of Troy —

ACHILLES. Who is this?

MENELAOS. This is our priest, Calchas.

ACHILLES. This guy is a priest?! He's a pretty good card player for a priest. You should see this guy play. He's amazing. He's got this one-handed shuffle. They teach you that in priest school?

MENELAOS. All right, settle down.

ACHILLES. *(Interrupting.)* Where do you get off making prophecies about me? You don't know me!

MENELAOS. He's trying to guide us.

CALCHAS. I am doing the best that I can.

ACHILLES. But you don't know any of this for certain!

CALCHAS. The study and practice of religion is not an exact science.

ACHILLES. See?!

MENELAOS. Wait a minute.

AGAMEMNON. What?

MENELAOS. What do you mean?

ACHILLES. He doesn't know anything for certain.

AGAMEMNON. Did God tell you that my daughter must be sacrificed or no?

CALCHAS. Great king, he did.

AGAMEMNON. You're certain?

CALCHAS. As certain as any man could be.

ACHILLES. Get a load of this guy.

AGAMEMNON. You're not one hundred percent on this?

CALCHAS. But, sir, that's not how a prophecy works.

AGAMEMNON. Then this could be a false prophecy. A trap, a mistake.

MENELAOS. It doesn't matter, it's too late.

AGAMEMNON. My God, I came this close, Menelaos.

MENELAOS. So what would you suggest we do instead? Sit around here and wait for what? For you to make up your mind. There has been a prophecy, and the girl is here. So it's not a hundred percent, but it's the best we've got.

AGAMEMNON. That's not good enough.

MENELAOS. The men have seen her. They expect action.

AGAMEMNON. But this may be the wrong action! He doesn't know.

MENELAOS. If you don't act now …

AGAMEMNON. Then what? What, Menelaos? *(Pause.)*
MENELAOS. Lead us.
AGAMEMNON. If I just had a sign.
CALCHAS. Agamemnon. God doesn't give you proof. He demands more from you than that. He asks you to have faith. I am only a priest. It is my duty to share his words with you. It is your duty to have faith. To hear his words and heed them. I believe He loves your daughter. I believe He has a great plan for her. Don't you see that? He is testing your love and obedience of him. And sometimes his path for us doesn't seem to make any sense here on Earth. But I believe in my soul, that he has great plans for us all.
CLYTEMNESTRA. I will not let you do this. *(Clytemnestra has appeared. She speaks slowly and deliberately.)* I will not let you do this.
CALCHAS. My lady, it is a heavy burden …
CLYTEMNESTRA. I will not let you do this.
CALCHAS. I …
CLYTEMNESTRA. Look me in my face. *(Pause.)* I will not let you do this.
MENELAOS. Dear sister. I love your daughter like my own.
CLYTEMNESTRA. Menelaos. You're behind this. I will not let you do this. What do you see in my face that frightens you?
MENELAOS. I am sorry for you.
CLYTEMNESTRA. You will be the sorry one.
AGAMEMNON. Leave us. *(They begin to exit.)*
CLYTEMNESTRA. I hope it doesn't come to that. *(They continue to exit.)*
AGAMEMNON. I meant to …
CLYTEMNESTRA. Do you actually believe that I would ever let you do this? Or that you would somehow manage to trick me and get away with it? She thinks she's getting married.
AGAMEMNON. I know. *(Pause.)*
CLYTEMNESTRA. Well?
AGAMEMNON. There was a prophecy.
CLYTEMNESTRA. Yes, I know about that and I couldn't care less. There are always prophecies. They said it would rain today. And look. How are you going to explain it to her? Or were you just planning to sneak up behind her and stab her in the back.
AGAMEMNON. Of course not.
CLYTEMNESTRA. Stab me in the back?
AGAMEMNON. This is a holy sacrifice.
CLYTEMNESTRA. Holy, holy, holy …

AGAMEMNON. There's a ritual of some kind — I don't know.
CLYTEMNESTRA. So you're still ironing out some of the details. You haven't decided yet whether or not to use an axe, a knife, a hammer.
AGAMEMNON. Please.
CLYTEMNESTRA. Poison perhaps.
AGAMEMNON. Do you think this is easy for me? You think I want this to happen, is that what you think of me?
CLYTEMNESTRA. I'm not sure I know who you are anymore.
(Iphigenia has entered.)
IPHIGENIA. Daddy.
CLYTEMNESTRA. However, whoever you are, I will not let you do this.
IPHIGENIA. What?
AGAMEMNON. I don't have a choice.
CLYTEMNESTRA. Then neither do I.
IPHIGENIA. What's going on?
CLYTEMNESTRA. Tell her. Tell her what you have in store for her.
AGAMEMNON. How can you do this?
CLYTEMNESTRA. Me?
AGAMEMNON. She's only a child.
IPHIGENIA. No I'm not.
CLYTEMNESTRA. Yes, it's so much better to get them when they're young and fresh.
AGAMEMNON. Enough.
CLYTEMNESTRA. Your father has a little surprise in mind for you. For your wedding. Don't you, dear.
IPHIGENIA. What is it?
AGAMEMNON. You're scaring her.
CLYTEMNESTRA. She should be scared! Tell her! Go on, tell your daughter how you're gonna do it.
IPHIGENIA. Daddy?
CLYTEMNESTRA. Isn't that sweet? She still thinks to call you Daddy. That's it, go to your father who loves you. He'll always protect you and no harm will come to you. Oh, come on. Be a man! If you ever loved your children, then tell her the truth. Say it to her face.
AGAMEMNON. I love my daughter.
CLYTEMNESTRA. Then promise not to kill her! Do it. Promise. Say something! Your father is silent. When it comes to protecting his family, your father has nothing to say.
AGAMEMNON. You hate me.

CLYTEMNESTRA. I haven't hated you since you killed my baby and my first husband.
IPHIGENIA. WHAT?!
AGAMEMNON. That was —
CLYTEMNESTRA. A war, he'll tell you. Men do strange things when they go to war. It's not all parades, banners, statues and flags. The men are not always handsome. Sometimes the men stick little babies up on pikes —
AGAMEMNON. Clytemnestra!
CLYTEMNESTRA. *(Over his lines.)* And they step on their skulls until the heads are split open!
IPHIGENIA. Mother!
AGAMEMNON. Enough!
CLYTEMNESTRA. *(Over their lines.)* And sometimes these great men will even slaughter their own little girls. Yes. Yes. Not many, but some. Or even one. It's enough. It just takes one father to slit his daughter's throat and that is quite enough to plant nightmares in the little heads of all the little girls of Greece. But it's a fine way to prove your faith in God.
AGAMEMNON. You know there is another side to this.
CLYTEMNESTRA. Don't tell me. Tell her. *(Agamemnon puts out a hand to Iphigenia but she pulls away.)*
IPHIGENIA. Am I getting married or not?
AGAMEMNON. Sweetheart. Sometimes we think one thing is going to happen and then something entirely unexpected happens instead.
IPHIGENIA. But — what's going to happen to me?
AGAMEMNON. God doesn't always make it clear what he wants of us.
IPHIGENIA. Well what do you think he wants?!
CLYTEMNESTRA. Tell her …
AGAMEMNON. You know how we're going to a very large war. It is a great and powerful army that we've assembled and yet God has stopped the wind.
IPHIGENIA. So the boats can't sail.
AGAMEMNON. That's right.
IPHIGENIA. What about rowing to Troy?
AGAMEMNON. We will row child, but we need the wind. It's too far to only row and too dangerous as well.
IPHIGENIA. If God took the wind out of the sails and stranded the army here in Aulis … then perhaps it is a sign that he doesn't

want this war. *(Short pause.)*
CLYTEMNESTRA. It's an interesting point.
AGAMEMNON. Darling this war means something important for the people of Greece. That we must protect our women.
IPHIGENIA. But how do you know that He really wants this war?
AGAMEMNON. We must have faith that there is a reason for what must happen.
CLYTEMNESTRA. TELL HER.
AGAMEMNON. God has demanded that I make a holy sacrifice in order for our journey to be blessed.
IPHIGENIA. Is it me? *(He cannot speak. She breaks down.)* But why?!
AGAMEMNON. Child …
IPHIGENIA. Stop saying that! If I'm old enough to be put to death, I'm not a child. What did you tell God?
AGAMEMNON. It doesn't matter what I tell him, it has to be done. *(He goes to take her physically.)*
IPHIGENIA. Noooo!
AGAMEMNON. Iphigenia, please.
IPHIGENIA. NOOOOO!!!
CLYTEMNESTRA. Listen to your daughter's screams.
IPHIGENIA. Don't touch me!
AGAMEMNON. They'll hear her!
CLYTEMNESTRA. Then let them hear her screams! *(Clytemnestra holds Iphigenia on the ground.)* Agamemnon. This is your daughter. Look at her. This is your own little girl. See her, she's right here. This is the girl we brought into the world and called Iphigenia. This is the girl who woke up crying in the night. This is the girl you held. You pet her and told her everything is going to be all right. Take her now. *(Agamemnon holds Iphigenia.)* You could never hurt her. You know this.
AGAMEMNON. I have no choice.
CLYTEMNESTRA. Look at me. I've loved you. You know it's true. We're your family. You would never harm us, any of us. You couldn't do that. This isn't you.
AGAMEMNON. You're right. It isn't. I could never do this. But the general must.
CLYTEMNESTRA. No. Darling, you'll regret this for the rest of your life. Send the army away and come home with us. I can make you happy again, I will. Just please don't do this. Let's go home and forget all about Aulis. We'll pretend none of this ever happened.

AGAMEMNON. Don't you think I want to do that?

CLYTEMNESTRA. Then do. Come home.

AGAMEMNON. This war is going to happen whether I want it to or not. It HAS to happen.

CLYTEMNESTRA. But why?!

AGAMEMNON. Because we're Greeks. We don't ask ourselves why we go to war. We ask ourselves why not.

CLYTEMNESTRA. You can't stop it, can you? You're not in charge anymore. You're nothing but a puppet. A silly little puppet.

AGAMEMNON. Don't you see, if I don't do this thing, they'll all come to me and to you and KILL ALL OF MY CHILDREN! Is that what you want?

CLYTEMNESTRA. While you're off in Troy, would you like me to dash the brains out of the rest of the children for you? Save you the trouble.

AGAMEMNON. You're a monster.

CLYTEMNESTRA. Don't make me so. *(Agamemnon gets up to leave.)*

IPHIGENIA. Daddy? Daddy. *(He stops but cannot turn back to look at her. He exits. Drums.)*

(Iphigenia runs on. The young woman gets up quickly.)

IPHIGENIA. Who are you? You frightened me. I didn't see you.

YOUNG WOMAN. Sorry.

IPHIGENIA. Where does that path lead?

YOUNG WOMAN. To the soldier's camp.

IPHIGENIA. And this one.

YOUNG WOMAN. Camp.

IPHIGENIA. Do they all lead back to camp?!

YOUNG WOMAN. It's a big camp.

IPHIGENIA. Will you help me? Please! They mustn't find me here. *(They face each other.)*

YOUNG WOMAN. I know who you are.

IPHIGENIA. If you tell them, I'll … They'll kill me! They mean to make a sacrifice of me to God. Because I'm a virgin! All my life they tell me to keep my virginity, that that's the most important thing. Yeah, well, great, look how this is turning out. My father. My own father has sold me to them. For wind. WIND. I can't believe he did that. The way he looked at me. As if I were already dead. God, I wish I were dead. I mean — not really. I just — I don't know what to do anymore. My own father! Damn him.

YOUNG WOMAN. What about your mother?

IPHIGENIA. Ohhhh, she is going to kill him for certain, you can count on that. She is going to carve him up into a thousand pieces and feed them to rats and pigs and … but I don't want him to die. I don't want any of this. Why can't we go back to before?

YOUNG WOMAN. *(Offering her a knife.)* Here, take this.

IPHIGENIA. What am I supposed to do with this?

YOUNG WOMAN. You could hide it and try to take one or two of them with you.

IPHIGENIA. I'm not going to kill anyone. *(Short pause.)*

YOUNG WOMAN. You said you were a virgin, right.

IPHIGENIA. I don't see how that is any of your —

YOUNG WOMAN. I'm just saying they typically like their sacrificial virgins to be … you know.

IPHIGENIA. Virgins.

YOUNG WOMAN. Plenty of soldiers in every direction.

IPHIGENIA. You mean I should go down that path and into the soldier's camp and just pick one of them out.

YOUNG WOMAN. It's a good idea.

IPHIGENIA. I've never done this before.

YOUNG WOMAN. He'll take care of most of the work, trust me. It probably won't take too long either.

IPHIGENIA. But what do I have to do, once I'm … you know?

YOUNG WOMAN. You won't have to do a thing. He'll take care of it. Just walk down this path right here and enter the first tent that you see. Then let out your hair, or loosen your clothes if you like. Believe me, he'll get the message.

IPHIGENIA. That I'm a whore.

YOUNG WOMAN. There are worse things. You were said to marry Achilles, right? Go and find his tent. Marry him tonight, in secret. Who will stop you? You were said to be his fiancée anyway.

IPHIGENIA. Would it even work?

YOUNG WOMAN. Tell the king after it's done.

IPHIGENIA. My father would kill me!

YOUNG WOMAN. He's going to kill you anyway.

IPHIGENIA. But I don't want him to hate me, I don't want to shame him or my family or — I don't want any of this! I can't just throw away my honor. I can't, I'm sorry. And I won't kill anyone. *(Pause.)*

YOUNG WOMAN. *(Offering her a knife.)* Then do it yourself. They can't sacrifice you if you're already dead. Listen to me, you

can stop this war. They can't sail without your sacrifice. Deny them. End it all right here and now. Let the Greeks remain in Greece. Think of it. One brief cut and the war will be over. Lives will be saved because of you.
IPHIGENIA. What about Troy?
YOUNG WOMAN. Forget Troy. Think of Greece.
IPHIGENIA. I want to believe you.
YOUNG WOMAN. Here. Take it. *(She hands her the sword. Iphigenia ponders. She touches the blade to her skin.)* End the war. You'll be a hero.
IPHIGENIA. I can't. I'm sorry I can't. *(She runs off.)*

(Achilles calls out from offstage.)
ACHILLES. I call upon the mighty Myrmidons! To arms! *(The puppet Myrmidons stumble forward from sleep and drunkenness.)*
MYRMIDON 2. Finally.
MYRMIDON 3. It's about time.
MYRMIDON 1. I hate going to arms.
MYRMIDON 2. I thought you hated waiting to go to arms.
MYRMIDON 1. Yes. Waiting is the worst.
ACHILLES. No matter. Arm yourself. There is a lady in need.
MYRMIDON 2. A needy lady.
MYRMIDON 1. I need a lady.
MYRMIDON 3. So we're finally going to get to see old Helen, eh.
ACHILLES. Well, no, actually. You see, we're not going to Troy, just yet.
MYRMIDON 1. What is this?!
MYRMIDON 2. Explain yourself!
MYRMIDON 3. Look, do we need to arm ourselves or not?
ACHILLES. Just a moment now. I am your general. If I say arm yourself, you arm yourself. If there's a lady in need, then there's a lady in need.
MYRMIDON 3. Who's the lady?
ACHILLES. My future wife.
MYRMIDON 3. Oh congratulations, sir.
MYRMIDON 2. We're getting married?
MYRMIDON 1. Marriage is the worst.
ACHILLES. I'm actually not getting married.
MYRMIDON 2. Good for you!
MYRMIDON 1. Screw marriage!
ACHILLES. Right. It's just that my fiancée is in a bit of trouble.

MYRMIDON 3. Got her pregnant, did you?
ACHILLES. No.
MYRMIDON 1. I love babies.
ACHILLES. It's quite another thing.
MYRMIDON 3. You mean her father wants to sacrifice her to appease God so that he'll put wind in the sails to launch the ships so we can go and ransack Troy?
ACHILLES. Why, yes. How did you know?
MYRMIDON 3. You said there wasn't a baby.
MYRMIDON 2. It had to be something.
ACHILLES. Right. Well done, Myrmidons.
MYRMIDONS. YAAAAY!
ACHILLES. Now we must stop Agamemnon from killing his daughter, my fiancée. To arms! *(He runs off alone. And returns.)* Well, come on then. What's the matter with you?
MYRMIDON 3. If your future wife isn't your fiancée, then who is your future wife?
ACHILLES. None of that matters now.
MYRMIDONS. Well, good, / That's a relief. / Take a load off. / Weight off my mind. *(They sit and begin taking off clothes to go back to bed.)*
ACHILLES. What are you doing?
MYRMIDON 3. You said it didn't matter. You're not getting married so there's no future wife to protect.
ACHILLES. It's true she was my future wife, only she's not anymore. But she still needs to be saved from her father.
MYRMIDON 3. But he's only sacrificing his daughter so we can get the ships blessed and go get Helen, yes?
ACHILLES. Yes.
MYRMIDON 3. So it's a good thing.
ACHILLES. Yes. No wrong!
MYRMIDON 2. Who's Helen again?
MYRMIDON 1. His future wife.
ACHILLES. No, no, no. You're wrong. Myrmidons, you must try and stay focused. *(Achilles explains in limerick. The Myrmidons keep time.)* He must sacrifice the girl, to appease God, to get the wind, to fill up the sails, to launch the ships, to sail across the sea, to knock down the walls and bring back Helen of Troy.
MYRMIDON 3. Yes, but what will happen if we save the girl?
ACHILLES. Well, nothing, I suppose.
MYRMIDON 3. No wind in the sails, eh?

ACHILLES. There could be.

MYRMIDON 3. What kind of general are you?!

MYRMIDON 2. Let's get Achilles!

MYRMIDON 1. I like getting Achilles.

ACHILLES. No, please stop! *(The puppets rouse themselves and chase Achilles off. Drums.)*

(The royal tent. Clytemnestra is frantically packing. Iphigenia wanders in.)

CLYTEMNESTRA. *(Putting a cloak on Iphigenia.)* Here, put this on.

IPHIGENIA. Mother, where are we going?

CLYTEMNESTRA. Let me protect you now, I'll explain the rest later. You'll have to trust me. Hide yourself. Put on men's clothing. We must blend in.

IPHIGENIA. But where will we go?

CLYTEMNESTRA. I don't know.

IPHIGENIA. Then what are we doing?

CLYTEMNESTRA. I don't know! All right, I don't know! All I know is you're about to be killed if you don't do as I say, now hurry up! *(Achilles rushes in.)*

ACHILLES. My lady. Things don't look very good.

CLYTEMNESTRA. Really. Where have you been? We could have used you here ten minutes ago.

ACHILLES. I was meeting with my men, the mighty Myrmidons, to plan your defense.

CLYTEMNESTRA. Well, where are they?

ACHILLES. They don't want to come.

CLYTEMNESTRA. What?

ACHILLES. When they learned that my errand was to protect your daughter — they tried to kill me.

CLYTEMNESTRA. Not all of them.

ACHILLES. All of them. These Greeks are ready to go to war and they don't want to wait any longer.

CLYTEMNESTRA. We've got to hurry.

ACHILLES. You can't escape. The king has given word that the roads be blocked.

CLYTEMNESTRA. I will kill that man today. I'm going to eat his heart!

IPHIGENIA. Mother. *(Achilles notices Iphigenia for the first time.)*

ACHILLES. You are Iphigenia.

IPHIGENIA. What's left of her. Hello.

ACHILLES. Hi. *(Pause.)* Tough day.

IPHIGENIA. A bit on the tough side. Yes.

ACHILLES. I'm sorry to meet you under these circumstances. But if by life or death I can save you, I will.

IPHIGENIA. How? You stand alone.

ACHILLES. I swear that I will slay any man who comes near you — whether it's only one man or five men, your father or ten thousand soldiers.

IPHIGENIA. But why would you do that?

ACHILLES. To save you.

IPHIGENIA. What would be the point of saving me if you had to kill everyone?

ACHILLES. Some principles are worth killing for.

IPHIGENIA. Worth killing every soldier of our country?

CLYTEMNESTRA. Iphigenia —

IPHIGENIA. What, Mother? Would you rather see Achilles kill the whole Greek army than see me sacrificed?

CLYTEMNESTRA. No question.

IPHIGENIA. The entire army. Think about it. They say there are a thousand ships right, or nearly. Fifty men per boat. That's fifty thousand men to be slain by this one man. This is your preference, Mother.

CLYTEMNESTRA. Yes.

IPHIGENIA. Fifty thousand bodies. I wonder what that looks like. Have you ever seen such a massacre?

ACHILLES. Fifty thousand. Never. Two thousand, maybe.

IPHIGENIA. Two thousand men. On the battlefield? What was that like?

ACHILLES. *(Slowly.)* It was — The entire hillside was covered with … you couldn't distinguish between … there were these layers …

IPHIGENIA. It must have been horrible for you.

ACHILLES. Unimaginable.

IPHIGENIA. And you would multiply that number by twenty-five. For me.

ACHILLES. I would.

IPHIGENIA. Then who would be left to protect Greece? Who would run the government, father the children, protect the women?

ACHILLES. Me?

IPHIGENIA. I am certain you are a mighty warrior, but even you cannot protect, manage, father and husband the entire country. *(Pause.)*

ACHILLES. You're wise. I would die to protect you.
CLYTEMNESTRA. We must find a way out / somehow.
IPHIGENIA. *(Over her lines.)* Mother.
CLYTEMNESTRA. There's got / to be something.
IPHIGENIA.

Mother, both of you listen to me.
Perhaps I was meant to die all along.
Everyone says it is the will of God. Maybe it is.
Achilles, you are kind, but I don't need your help. Besides,
Greece needs you for our war on Troy. That's what you have to
do. My destiny lies here in Aulis.

I've made up my mind to die for my country.
It is an honor to die in battle.
Women rarely gain such an honor.

So here I stand, a girl.
Not quite a woman really.
And all the strength of Greece looks to me. To me.
All those ships, all these soldiers, the entire nation
Looks to me.
I am the one who will protect our women.
I am the one who will make the barbarians fear the revenge of
Greece.
I am the one.
And all I have to do is die? My life.
It's a small price to pay to gain so much in return.

You're my mother. You gave birth to me, for this.
Look around you, they're all here.
Greece is *here!*
They've all left their homes, their families, their ways of life.
They risk their lives.
Not just for Helen.
But because Troy hurt our country.
And we can't allow that to happen. Not now, not ever again.
I won't allow it.

Like everyone else here who has bravely pledged an oath to
defend our country, I will humbly take my place and stand with
them, if they'll have me.

If my life will fill the sails of our fleet,
If my life will help to defend our land,
If my life is needed by Greece,
Then take it.

That's how I want to be remembered.
This will be my wedding, my children, my moment.
Greece is the greatest country in the world.
If we were truly meant to rule this world.
We have to do it now.
(Pause.)
ACHILLES. If I could have you for my wife … well, I'd really like that. You really are such a noble creature for a girl so young, so …
IPHIGENIA. I'm not that young.
ACHILLES. I didn't mean *too* young. You're perfect. It's just that — they are planning to *kill you.*
IPHIGENIA. I know. Perhaps it will be quick.
CLYTEMNESTRA. Nooooo.
ACHILLES. I see your mind is made up.
IPHIGENIA. It is.
ACHILLES. Because I'll be there. Right there by your side at the altar. You just say the word and I'll …
IPHIGENIA. Kill everyone in sight.
ACHILLES. Yes.
IPHIGENIA. I'll be all right. One thing. I know we're not getting married … *(She kisses him.)* Sorry.
ACHILLES. You're sure —
IPHIGENIA. I'm sure. Goodbye. *(He starts to go, a trifle flustered.)*
ACHILLES. I'll — I'll see you later. At the …
IPHIGENIA. Human sacrifice.
ACHILLES. Right. Until then. *(He goes.)*
IPHIGENIA. Mother, don't cry. Please, Mother, I want you to be proud.
CLYTEMNESTRA. I've always been proud of you.
IPHIGENIA. Of what I'm doing.
CLYTEMNESTRA. How can I be?
IPHIGENIA. Mother, please!
CLYTEMNESTRA. No, you listen to me, young lady. You don't know what you're asking. You don't have any children, but when you do — Oh my God, you'll never know. What it's like to see your child suffer, when your baby has a head cold or a bloody knee,

or even a broken heart. But to see your child die?
IPHIGENIA. I have a reason.
CLYTEMNESTRA. IT'S NOT YOUR REASON! And you're not in charge of your life! I am your mother, and I don't care what is right or what the war is, I don't. Just don't ask me to gladly accept the death of my eldest daughter.
IPHIGENIA. Please Mother, I need your support. And no mourning. Don't you mourn me. This is a good thing. No vigils, no black robes, no tears. This is a celebration. *(Pause.)* Mother, I need you to promise not to hate my father. This is my decision. *(The young woman enters.)*
YOUNG WOMAN. They are coming.
IPHIGENIA. Where am I supposed to go? I hope they don't send a bunch of soldiers to grab me. Do they know I go willingly? *(Clytemnestra clings to her.)*
CLYTEMNESTRA. I am coming with you.
IPHIGENIA. No! I can't have you there.
CLYTEMNESTRA. I won't let go of you!
IPHIGENIA. I don't want you to see this. I won't be able to do this with you watching me. Mother, please let go. I'm going to do this. *(To young woman.)* Will you help me?
YOUNG WOMAN. If you want me to.
IPHIGENIA. Come, wrap me up in my wedding gown. *(The young woman takes some fabric and begins to wrap her in it.)* This is fitting. For I will be made the bride of Greece. I was made to conquer Troy. I will fill the sails at sea. And I will see the barbarous skulls rotting on the pikes of the walls of Troy. *(Armed soldiers appear.)*
SOLDIER. My lady. It's time.
IPHIGENIA. I'm ready.
CLYTEMNESTRA. Take me. A mother's right.
IPHIGENIA. What are you doing?
CLYTEMNESTRA. I stand here for her. Whatever you wish to do to her, do it to me.
IPHIGENIA. Mother.
SOLDIER. We have orders.
CLYTEMNESTRA. I'm giving the orders now. You will take me in her place.
IPHIGENIA. It's not you they need.
CLYTEMNESTRA. You will do it.
IPHIGENIA. Mother, I've got to go.
CLYTEMNESTRA. I command you to take me!

YOUNG WOMAN. *(Softly.)* You …
SOLDIER. I'm sorry. *(They take Iphigenia by her arms.)*
CLYTEMNESTRA. Don't touch her!
IPHIGENIA. Goodbye, Mother.
CLYTEMNESTRA. You let go of her!
SOLDIER. Come!
CLYTEMNESTRA. Let go of my daughter!
IPHIGENIA. *(Interrupting.)* Mother, it's all right. Hold on. It's going to be all right.
CLYTEMNESTRA. Nooo.
IPHIGENIA. We're gonna win this war!

(They go. Clytemnestra laments. Drums increase. Music. Eventually, the young woman holds Clytemnestra. The ceremony begins. At the same time in the background, we see the altar rising up high in silhouette. A garland is placed around Iphigenia's head as she bows and takes the arm of Agamemnon. Slowly, they rise up the stairs of the altar. Calchas appears. Agamemnon kisses his daughter on her forehead. They squeeze hands, and she nods before kneeling down. Her top is lowered, exposing her naked shoulders. A large knife is unsheathed and raised high into the air. Iphigenia gasps.)
CLYTEMNESTRA. *(Quietly rocking.)* Noooooooooooooooooo … *(As the knife goes down, the lights shift drastically and Iphigenia has vanished. A bloody deer sits on the altar, dripping down the stairs. People are confused.)*
VOICES. Did it work? / What has happened? / Where's the girl? / Is it a trick? *(The soldiers begin to get violent when gales of wind begin to blow.)*
CALCHAS. You men of Greece, God has placed this deer on the altar, for he is honored by the sacrifice of this noble girl and does not wish his altar to be defiled by such a noble blood, lovingly offered. Take comfort and leave Aulis now. To your ships! To sea! For your journey has been blessed and the wind will rise to meet you! *(Soldiers enter cheering and singing as others begin rushing on with equipment, swords, etc., to load the ships. The lines overlap in the general tumult which ensues in the rush to war.)*
ALL.
> To war!
> To battle!
> Get these to the ship!
> Come on, we're getting out of here!

Die Trojans die!
All of them?
As many as you can carry, we're gonna need them later!
Come on, we've got to hurry.
The ships will launch in two minutes.
The wind is high, but the tide won't wait.
ACHILLES. Myrmidons, to arms, to the ships — really, this time.
Everybody up! Let's hurry now.
ALL.
> Let's go!
> Get a move on!
> Did you see the girl?
> It was amazing!
> Never doubt a true king.
> It was a miracle.

(A bloody Agamemnon stands near the ships, attended.)
AGAMEMNON. My daughter is gone to a better place! She is gone
but not forgotten. Iphigenia, our first casualty of the war on Troy.
> Our fallen hero.
> Our daughter.
> Our nation's daughter.
> She believed in you
> In our cause
> She believed in Greece and what it stands for.
> And she did not just say so, no.
> Words were too small for her.
> She stepped forward and said, "Take me!"
> I am not afraid.
> I am not afraid to stand up for my people,
> I am not afraid to die for my country,
> I am not afraid of war,
> Or God,
> Or death,
> Or Troy,
> I am not afraid!"
>
> She gave her life
> To protect our freedom.
> Will you do the same?!
> Will you stand with her and take up arms with her?!
ALL. YES!

AGAMEMNON. Will you fight with her? Shed blood with her?!
ALL. YES!
AGAMEMNON. Will you die with her?!
ALL. YES!
AGAMEMNON. Iphigenia!
ALL. IPHIGENIA!
AGAMEMNON. Farewell Greece! Until we meet again! Now for
Troy! To retrieve the virtuous Helen!
ALL. HELEN! (*All depart on great ships except Clytemnestra. The
soldiers wield swords and spears, as does Clytemnestra.*)
SOLDIERS. (*Singing the march with a chorus of a thousand voices.*)
   WE'RE OFF TO KILL THE TROJANS
   TO RECLAIM MENELAOS' BRIDE
   THE VIRTUOUS LADY HELEN
   FOR WHOM OUR COUNTRY CRIED

   BEWARE YOU TROJAN COWARDS
   YOU HAD BETTER RUN AND HIDE
   THE GREEKS ARRIVE ON YOUR SHORES
   TO RETRIEVE OUR NATION'S BRIDE.

   ACHILLES OUR GREAT HERO
   WILL THROW HIS MIGHTY SPEAR
   AND PIERCE THE ARMOR OF HECTOR
   AND YANK OLD PRIAM'S BEARD

   FOR WE'RE FIGHTING FOR OUR FREEDOM
   WE'RE FIGHTING FOR OUR PRIDE
   THE GREEKS ARRIVE ON YOUR SHORES
   WE WON'T LEAVE 'TIL YOUR PEOPLE HAVE DIED!

End of Play

PROPERTY LIST

Camp equipment, swords, spears
Sword, blade sharpener
Letter
Knife
Clothing
Swords, knives
Knife
Altar, bloody deer

SOUND EFFECTS

Twig snaps
Drums
Music
Wind

NEW PLAYS

★ **THE EXONERATED by Jessica Blank and Erik Jensen.** Six interwoven stories paint a picture of an American criminal justice system gone horribly wrong and six brave souls who persevered to survive it. "The #1 play of the year...intense and deeply affecting..." *–NY Times.* "Riveting. Simple, honest storytelling that demands reflection." *–A.P.* "Artful and moving...pays tribute to the resilience of human hearts and minds." *–Variety.* "Stark...riveting...cunningly orchestrated." *–The New Yorker.* "Hard-hitting, powerful, and socially relevant." *–Hollywood Reporter.* [7M, 3W] ISBN: 0-8222-1946-8

★ **STRING FEVER by Jacquelyn Reingold.** Lily juggles the big issues: turning forty, artificial insemination and the elusive scientific Theory of Everything in this Off-Broadway comedy hit. "Applies the elusive rules of string theory to the conundrums of one woman's love life. Think *Sex and the City* meets *Copenhagen*." *–NY Times.* "A funny offbeat and touching look at relationships...an appealing romantic comedy populated by oddball characters." *–NY Daily News.* "Where kooky, zany, and madcap meet...whimsically winsome." *–NY Magazine.* "STRING FEVER will have audience members happily stringing along." *–TheaterMania.com.* "Reingold's language is surprising, inventive, and unique." *–nytheatre.com.* "...[a] whimsical comic voice." *–Time Out.* [3M, 3W (doubling)] ISBN: 0-8222-1952-2

★ **DEBBIE DOES DALLAS adapted by Erica Schmidt, composed by Andrew Sherman, conceived by Susan L. Schwartz.** A modern morality tale told as a comic musical of tragic proportions as the classic film is brought to the stage. "A scream! A saucy, tongue-in-cheek romp." *–The New Yorker.* "Hilarious! DEBBIE manages to have it all: beauty, brains and a great sense of humor!" *–Time Out.* "Shamelessly silly, shrewdly self-aware and proud of being naughty. Great fun!" *–NY Times.* "Racy and raucous, a lighthearted, fast-paced thoroughly engaging and hilarious send-up." *–NY Daily News.* [3M, 5W] ISBN: 0-8222-1955-7

★ **THE MYSTERY PLAYS by Roberto Aguirre-Sacasa.** Two interrelated one acts, loosely based on the tradition of the medieval mystery plays. "... stylish, spine-tingling...Mr. Aguirre-Sacasa uses standard tricks of horror stories, borrowing liberally from masters like Kafka, Lovecraft, Hitchock...But his mastery of the genre is his own...irresistible." *–NY Times.* "Undaunted by the special-effects limitations of theatre, playwright and *Marvel* comic-book writer Roberto Aguirre-Sacasa maps out some creepy twilight zones in THE MYSTERY PLAYS, an engaging, related pair of one acts...The theatre may rarely deliver shocks equivalent to, say, *Dawn of the Dead*, but Aguirre-Sacasa's work is fine compensation." *–Time Out.* [4M, 2W] ISBN: 0-8222-2038-5

★ **THE JOURNALS OF MIHAIL SEBASTIAN by David Auburn.** This epic one-man play spans eight tumultuous years and opens a uniquely personal window on the Romanian Holocaust and the Second World War. "Powerful." *–NY Times.* "[THE JOURNALS OF MIHAIL SEBASTIAN] allows us to glimpse the idiosyncratic effects of that awful history on one intelligent, pragmatic, recognizably real man..." *–NY Newsday.* [3M, 5W] ISBN: 0-8222-2006-7

★ **LIVING OUT by Lisa Loomer.** The story of the complicated relationship between a Salvadoran nanny and the Anglo lawyer she works for. "A stellar new play. Searingly funny." *–The New Yorker.* "Both generous and merciless, equally enjoyable and disturbing." *–NY Newsday.* "A bitingly funny new comedy. The plight of working mothers is explored from two pointedly contrasting perspectives in this sympathetic, sensitive new play." *–Variety.* [2M, 6W] ISBN: 0-8222-1994-8

DRAMATISTS PLAY SERVICE, INC.
440 Park Avenue South, New York, NY 10016 212-683-8960 Fax 212-213-1539
postmaster@dramatists.com www.dramatists.com

NEW PLAYS

★ **MATCH by Stephen Belber.** Mike and Lisa Davis interview a dancer and choreographer about his life, but it is soon evident that their agenda will either ruin or inspire them— and definitely change their lives forever. "Prolific laughs and ear-to-ear smiles." –*NY Magazine.* "Uproariously funny, deeply moving, enthralling theater. Stephen Belber's MATCH has great beauty and tenderness, and abounds in wit." –*NY Daily News.* "Three and a half out of four stars." –*USA Today.* "A theatrical steeplechase that leads straight from outrageous bitchery to unadorned, heartfelt emotion." –*Wall Street Journal.* [2M, 1W] ISBN: 0-8222-2020-2

★ **HANK WILLIAMS: LOST HIGHWAY by Randal Myler and Mark Harelik.** The story of the beloved and volatile country-music legend Hank Williams, featuring twenty-five of his most unforgettable songs. "[LOST HIGHWAY has] the exhilarating feeling of Williams on stage in a particular place on a particular night…serves up classic country with the edges raw and the energy hot…By the end of the play, you've traveled on a profound emotional journey: LOST HIGHWAY transports its audience and communicates the inspiring message of the beauty and richness of Williams' songs…forceful, clear-eyed, moving, impressive." –*Rolling Stone.* "…honors a very particular musical talent with care and energy… smart, sweet, poignant." –*NY Times.* [7M, 3W] ISBN: 0-8222-1985-9

★ **THE STORY by Tracey Scott Wilson.** An ambitious black newspaper reporter goes against her editor to investigate a murder and finds the *best* story…but at what cost? "A singular new voice…deeply emotional, deeply intellectual, and deeply musical…" –*The New Yorker.* "…a conscientious and absorbing new drama…" –*NY Times.* "…a riveting, tough-minded drama about race, reporting and the truth…" –*A.P.* "… a stylish, attention-holding script that ends on a chilling note that will leave viewers with much to talk about." –*Curtain Up.* [2M, 7W (doubling, flexible casting)] ISBN: 0-8222-1998-0

★ **OUR LADY OF 121st STREET by Stephen Adly Guirgis.** The body of Sister Rose, beloved Harlem nun, has been stolen, reuniting a group of life-challenged childhood friends who square off as they wait for her return. "A scorching and dark new comedy… Mr. Guirgis has one of the finest imaginations for dialogue to come along in years." –*NY Times.* "Stephen Guirgis may be the best playwright in America under forty." –*NY Magazine.* [8M, 4W] ISBN: 0-8222-1965-4

★ **HOLLYWOOD ARMS by Carrie Hamilton and Carol Burnett.** The coming-of-age story of a dreamer who manages to escape her bleak life and follow her romantic ambitions to stardom. Based on Carol Burnett's bestselling autobiography, *One More Time.* "…pure theatre and pure entertainment…" –*Talkin' Broadway.* "…a warm, fuzzy evening of theatre." –*BrodwayBeat.com.* "…chuckles and smiles of recognition or surprise flow naturally…a remarkable slice of life." –*TheatreScene.net.* [5M, 5W, 1 girl] ISBN: 0-8222-1959-X

★ **INVENTING VAN GOGH by Steven Dietz.** A haunting and hallucinatory drama about the making of art, the obsession to create and the fine line that separates truth from myth. "Like a van Gogh painting, Dietz's story is a gorgeous example of excess—one that remakes reality with broad, well-chosen brush strokes. At evening's end, we're left with the author's resounding opinions on art and artifice, and provoked by his constant query into which is greater: van Gogh's art or his violent myth." –*Phoenix New Times.* "Dietz's writing is never simple. It is always brilliant. Shaded, compressed, direct, lucid—he frames his subject with a remarkable understanding of painting as a physical experience." –*Tucson Citizen.* [4M, 1W] ISBN: 0-8222-1954-9

DRAMATISTS PLAY SERVICE, INC.
440 Park Avenue South, New York, NY 10016 212-683-8960 Fax 212-213-1539
postmaster@dramatists.com www.dramatists.com

NEW PLAYS

★ **INTIMATE APPAREL by Lynn Nottage.** The moving and lyrical story of a turn-of-the-century black seamstress whose gifted hands and sewing machine are the tools she uses to fashion her dreams from the whole cloth of her life's experiences. "...Nottage's play has a delicacy and eloquence that seem absolutely right for the time she is depicting..." –*NY Daily News.* "...thoughtful, affecting...The play offers poignant commentary on an era when the cut and color of one's dress—and of course, skin—determined whom one could and could not marry, sleep with, even talk to in public." –*Variety.* [2M, 4W] ISBN: 0-8222-2009-1

★ **BROOKLYN BOY by Donald Margulies.** A witty and insightful look at what happens to a writer when his novel hits the bestseller list. "The characters are beautifully drawn, the dialogue sparkles..." –*nytheatre.com.* "Few playwrights have the mastery to smartly investigate so much through a laugh-out-loud comedy that combines the vintage subject matter of successful writer-returning-to-ethnic-roots with the familiar mid-life crisis." –*Show Business Weekly.* [4M, 3W] ISBN: 0-8222-2074-1

★ **CROWNS by Regina Taylor.** Hats become a springboard for an exploration of black history and identity in this celebratory musical play. "Taylor pulls off a Hat Trick: She scores thrice, turning CROWNS into an artful amalgamation of oral history, fashion show, and musical theater..." –*TheatreMania.com.* "...wholly theatrical...Ms. Taylor has created a show that seems to arise out of spontaneous combustion, as if a bevy of department-store customers simultaneously decided to stage a revival meeting in the changing room." –*NY Times.* [1M, 6W (2 musicians)] ISBN: 0-8222-1963-8

★ **EXITS AND ENTRANCES by Athol Fugard.** The story of a relationship between a young playwright on the threshold of his career and an aging actor who has reached the end of his. "[Fugard] can say more with a single line than most playwrights convey in an entire script...Paraphrasing the title, it's safe to say this drama, making its memorable entrance into our consciousness, is unlikely to exit as long as a theater exists for exceptional work." –*Variety.* "A thought-provoking, elegant and engrossing new play..." –*Hollywood Reporter.* [2M] ISBN: 0-8222-2041-5

★ **BUG by Tracy Letts.** A thriller featuring a pair of star-crossed lovers in an Oklahoma City motel facing a bug invasion, paranoia, conspiracy theories and twisted psychological motives. "...obscenely exciting...top-flight craftsmanship. Buckle up and brace yourself..." –*NY Times.* "...[a] thoroughly outrageous and thoroughly entertaining play...the possibility of enemies, real and imagined, to squash has never been more theatrical." –*A.P.* [3M, 2W] ISBN: 0-8222-2016-4

★ **THOM PAIN (BASED ON NOTHING) by Will Eno.** An ordinary man muses on childhood, yearning, disappointment and loss, as he draws the audience into his last-ditch plea for empathy and enlightenment. "It's one of those treasured nights in the theater—treasured nights anywhere, for that matter—that can leave you both breathless with exhilaration and...in a puddle of tears." –*NY Times.* "Eno's words...are familiar, but proffered in a way that is constantly contradictory to our expectations. Beckett is certainly among his literary ancestors." –*nytheatre.com.* [1M] ISBN: 0-8222-2076-8

★ **THE LONG CHRISTMAS RIDE HOME by Paula Vogel.** Past, present and future collide on a snowy Christmas Eve for a troubled family of five. "...[a] lovely and hauntingly original family drama...a work that breathes so much life into the theater." –*Time Out.* "...[a] delicate visual feast..." –*NY Times.* "...brutal and lovely...the overall effect is magical." –*NY Newsday.* [3M, 3W] ISBN: 0-8222-2003-2

DRAMATISTS PLAY SERVICE, INC.
440 Park Avenue South, New York, NY 10016 212-683-8960 Fax 212-213-1539
postmaster@dramatists.com www.dramatists.com